Our Changing World

THE TIMELINE LIBRARY

THE HISTORY OF THE COMPUTER

BY BARBARA A. SOMERVILL

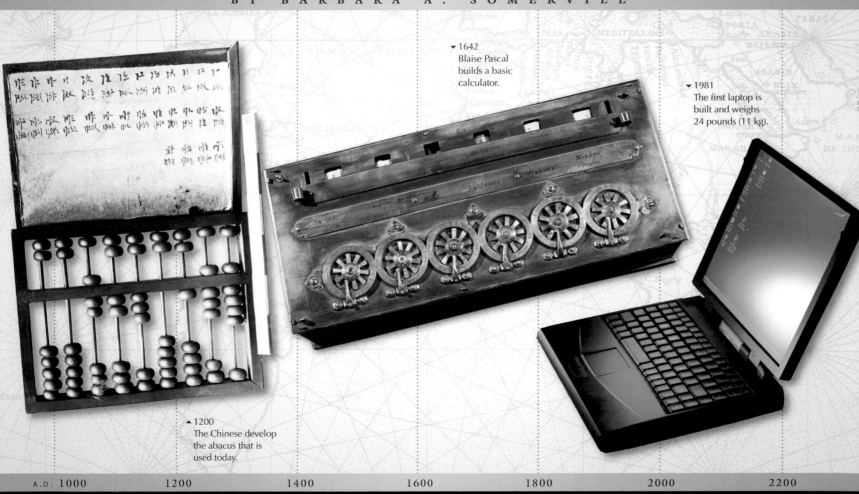

▼ 1642
Blaise Pascal
builds a basic
calculator.

▼ 1981
The first laptop is
built and weighs
24 pounds (11 kg).

▲ 1200
The Chinese develop
the abacus that is
used today.

| A.D. 1000 | 1200 | 1400 | 1600 | 1800 | 2000 | 2200 |

Content Adviser: Paul Ceruzzi, Curator, Smithsonian Institution, Washington, D.C.

THE CHILD'S WORLD® • CHANHASSEN, MINNESOTA

The Child's World®

Published in the United States of America by The Child's World®
PO Box 326 • Chanhassen, MN 55317-0326 • 800-599-READ • www.childsworld.com

ACKNOWLEDGMENTS
The Child's World®: Mary Berendes, Publishing Director

Editorial Directions, Inc.: E. Russell Primm, Editorial Director; Katie Marsico, Managing Editor and Line Editor; Judith Shiffer, Assistant Editor; Rory Mabin and Caroline Wood, Editorial Assistants; Susan Hindman, Copy Editor; Jennifer Martin, Proofreader; Judith Frisbee, Peter Garnham, Olivia Nellums, Chris Simms, and Stephen Carl Wender, Fact Checkers; Tim Griffin/IndexServ, Indexer; Cian Loughlin O'Day, Photo Researcher; Linda S. Koutris, Photo Selector

The Design Lab: Kathleen Petelinsek, Design and Art Production

PHOTOS
Cover / frontispiece: left—Bettmann/Corbis; center—Archivo Iconografico, S.A./Corbis; right—Corbis.

Interior: 5—Julie Houck/Corbis; 7—The Granger Collection; 8, 12, 15—Bettmann/Corbis; 9—Gustano Tomsich/ Corbis; 10—Burke/Triolo Productions/Brand X Pictures/Getty Images; 14—Hulton-Deutsch Collection/Corbis; 16, 25—Computer History Museum; 18—Corbis; 21—Texas Instruments/Reuters/Corbis; 23—Charles E. Rotkin; 24— Kim Kulish/Corbis; 27—NASA/JSC; 28—Wolfgang Rattay/Reuters/Corbis.

LIBRARY OF CONGRESS CATALOGING-IN-PUBLICATION DATA
Somervill, Barbara A.
  The history of the computer / by Barbara Somervill.
    p. cm. — (Our Changing World—The Timeline Library)
  Includes index.
  ISBN 1-59296-437-0 (library bound : alk. paper)
  1. Computers—History—Juvenile literature. I. Title. II. Series.
  QA76.52.S6 2006
  004—dc22   2005024781

TABLE OF CONTENTS

100101000111 . . .

The students squirmed in their seats. It was computer lab time, and they wanted to get busy. Mrs. Winslow wrote on the board:

100101000111010101010101010001101000 . . .

She turned to the class. "Julio, what do you think this says?"

Julio read the numbers aloud: "100101000 . . ."

"Yes," said Mrs. Winslow, "they are ones and zeros, but what do they mean?" The class was puzzled. What could they mean besides ones and zeros?

"Suppose you used a light switch. How would you use it to show the ones and zeros?" asked Mrs. Winslow.

Hands shot up into the air. "The 'on' is one, and the 'off' is zero," said Tyrell. Mrs. Winslow smiled. "Exactly. With electricity, there can only be two signals: on and off."

Julio raised his hand. "But what does that have to do with computers?"

"Every game, everything you write, every **calculation,** picture, video, or song on your computer is made up of millions . . . no, billions of ones and

Every action performed on a computer involves billions of electronic signals.

zeros, signals that say on and off. Okay, class, turn on your computers," said

Mrs. Winslow. "Let's put those ones and zeros to work."

ABACUS AND SLIDE RULES

Early humans needed to count things long before they had words for numbers. They counted using their fingers and sometimes even their toes. But twenty was not a big enough number when counting sheep in a herd or baskets of grain.

As families grew into communities, counting became more important. How many people lived in the village? How many men could serve as soldiers? How much tax money needed to be collected? Early cultures soon developed methods of counting and recording numbers.

CA. 3000 B.C.: THE ABACUS AND COUNTING TABLES

Mystery surrounds the origin of the **abacus.** Some historians believe the Chinese invented the abacus in about 3000 B.C. Others think the abacus got its

ca. 3000 B.C.	500 B.C.
The abacus is invented in either China or Babylonia.	A bead-and-wire abacus is developed in Egypt.
Athens develops as an early Greek city.	King Darius I of Persia declares that Aramaic is the official language of the western part of his kingdom.

start in Babylonia. An Egyptian bead-and-wire abacus from 500 B.C. is very similar to a Chinese abacus from the same period. The Romans used a device called a *calculi,* which was also like an abacus.

A counting table, like an abacus, was a simple aid for adding and subtracting. Early counting tables were wooden trays filled with sand. A person used a stick to mark units in the sand. But sand counting tables had an obvious drawback—one shake and the calculation disappeared.

Sand tables evolved into tables carved with grooves, or lines, and hollows. Twigs and stones marked units of ten and above. Many different cultures developed counting tables, including the Romans, Greeks, and Egyptians.

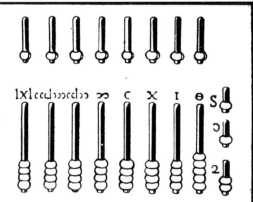

Romans develop a hand-held abacus (right).

ca. A.D. 100

The first Chinese dictionary is compiled.

7

In A.D. 1200, the Chinese developed another abacus, one that is often seen in elementary schools today. This classic Chinese abacus has two sections: the upper "heaven" section and the lower "Earth" section. Marker positions indicate number values. The upper section of a Chinese abacus contains two beads on each wire, while the lower section has five beads per wire. Using both sections, a person can compute numbers up to the millions.

The abacus and counting table helped early people perform calculations. But these inventions were unable to solve more complicated mathematical problems.

The Chinese develop the abacus that is used today (left).

A.D. 1200

The empire of Mali flourishes in northern Africa.

1622: SLIDE RULES

By the 1600s, mathematics had advanced far beyond counting on their fingers. The Greeks and Arabs had developed geometry and algebra centuries earlier. Geometry is math that deals with lines, angles, and shapes. Algebra uses letters and symbols to represent unknown numbers. But mathematicians still had a long way to go. Calculations such as figuring out the distance from the Moon to the Earth required complicated math.

Londoner William Oughtred was a minister and a mathematician. Historians credit Oughtred with introducing the idea of using x to mean

QUIPUS

THE INCAS OF PERU HAD NO WRITTEN LANGUAGE. THEY RECORDED NUMBERS RELATED TO POPULATION, CROPS, AND TAXES ON *QUIPUS*. QUIPUS WERE PATTERNS OF KNOTS MADE WITH COLORED YARN. EACH KNOT STYLE INDICATED A NUMBER. EACH COLOR REFERRED TO THE ITEM BEING COUNTED.

ca. 1609

The telescope (right) is first used for astronomy by Galileo.

"multiply." Oughtred thought he could develop a better, more accurate way of doing difficult math.

In 1622, Oughtred and his student Richard Delamain worked on developing the circular **slide rule.** Both men took credit for the invention. Which one actually did the inventing doesn't matter. The slide rule served as an early type of calculator, but it was not a computer.

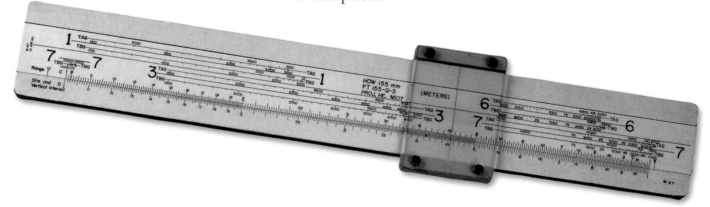

Either Williams Oughtred or Richard Delamain creates the first slide rule (above).

1622

Explorer Henry Hudson enters New York Bay.

CHAPTER TWO

EARLY COMPUTERS

H ere's a riddle: What do a tax collector's son, a weaver, and the U.S. **Census** have in common? Easy—they were all important to the development of the computer.

In 1642, Frenchman Blaise Pascal built a mechanical calculator to help his father figure out how much tax money people owed the government. Pascal was a brilliant mathematician, but his invention failed. Within ten years, Pascal made at least fifty different **prototypes** of his calculator, but few people were interested.

French money, unlike Pascal's calculator, was not based on units of ten. One *livre* equaled twenty *sols*. Twelve *deniers* equaled one *sol*. Calculating money on Pascal's machine, called a Pascaline, was nearly impossible. Still,

Blaise Pascal builds a basic calculator.

1642

Mathematician and physicist Isaac Newton is born.

Pascal proved that a machine could do complicated calculations. This was a giant step toward creating a computer.

The next important event occurred in a French factory. In 1801, Joseph-Marie Jacquard wanted to weave patterns into cloth. He developed a system of punch cards to make looms weave the patterns. As wooden rods moved through the holes in the cards, parts of the loom moved. With each movement, a new part of a pattern was produced.

About thirty years later, Englishman

Joseph-Marie Jacquard develops a system of punch cards to guide a loom (left).

1801

Thomas Jefferson becomes president of the United States.

Charles Babbage learned about Jacquard's punch-card loom. In 1833, Babbage tried using punch cards to make a simple computer. He designed the Analytical Engine to perform mathematical calculations. Babbage was on the right track, but he never got around to building a successful model. Still, he determined that a computer needed four basic elements: input (punch cards), a memory, a processor, and a means to output the result.

More than fifty years later, Herman Hollerith developed an automatic punch-card calculator. Hollerith figured out how to convert the information on punched cards into electrical impulses. In turn, these impulses triggered mechanical counters.

"ON TWO OCCASIONS I HAVE BEEN ASKED, 'PRAY, MR. BABBAGE, IF YOU PUT INTO THE MACHINE WRONG FIGURES, WILL THE RIGHT ANSWERS COME OUT?' I AM NOT ABLE . . . TO [UNDERSTAND] THE KIND OF CONFUSION OF IDEAS THAT COULD PROVOKE SUCH A QUESTION."
—CHARLES BABBAGE

Charles Babbage designs the Analytical Engine.

The American Anti-Slavery Society is created in Philadelphia, Pennsylvania.

The U.S. government was impressed. Hollerith was hired to build an electronic machine that used punch cards to count the U.S. Census. Hollerith's census counter developed into a major business. Today, it is called International Business Machines (IBM).

Now all that was needed was to put everything together and create a computer. Well, a *few* more advancements were necessary. For example, Vladimir Zworykin invented the cathode ray tube in 1928. The tube was an early television—an ancestor of today's computer monitor.

Herman Hollerith builds an electronic machine (left) to count the U.S. Census.

1890

Idaho and Wyoming gain statehood.

CHAPTER THREE

ENIAC

Just who built the first computer is a question with many answers. Several people believe that Konrad Zuse, a German engineer, produced the first real computer—the Z1—in 1936. He said, "I was too lazy to calculate, and so [I] invented the computer."

Zuse's invention could do a week's worth of math work in just a few hours. At that time, Germany was getting ready for World War II (1939–1945). The German government used Zuse's invention to help their war effort. As the war came to an end, the Germans took Zuse's Z4 model and hid it in a stable so enemy forces couldn't use it. The Z4 remained hidden until after the war ended.

In the United States, several scientists also worked to create a computer during the 1940s. John Atanasoff and Clifford Berry developed the ABC

1936

Konrad Zuse invents the Z1.

Francisco Franco (right) is elected head of state in Spain.

Computer in 1942. At Harvard University in Cambridge, Massachusetts, Howard Aiken and Grace Hopper worked on the Mark 1 computer. And the U.S. Army hired John Mauchly and J. Presper Eckert to build a calculating machine. Army officials wanted to calculate firing solutions for large weapons and missiles.

Mauchly and Eckert worked at the University of Pennsylvania in Philadelphia, Pennsylvania. It took them a year to design ENIAC (Electronic Numeric Integrator and Computer). Another eighteen months passed while they built the computer. They finished ENIAC in the fall of 1945, after World War II was already over. They received a **patent** for the computer on June 26, 1947.

16

1942

John Atanasoff and Clifford Berry develop the ABC Computer (left).

Enrico Fermi and his colleagues carry out the first controlled nuclear reaction.

Building ENIAC cost $500,000. Several thousand components, or parts, were necessary to control the computer's flow of electricity. Today, **silicon chips** the size of thumbnails have replaced all of the various tubes and electrical components that were used to make ENIAC.

In addition to having lots of parts, ENIAC took up 1,800 square feet (167 sq meters) and weighed 30 tons. When it was turned on, the computer required so much power that it threw most of Philadelphia into darkness.

ENIAC could add 5,000 numbers or multiply fourteen ten-digit numbers in one second. In 1947, that was extremely fast. Yet, ENIAC had less power and speed than a $10 calculator does today.

> "COMPUTERS ARE USELESS. THEY CAN ONLY GIVE YOU ANSWERS."
> —PABLO PICASSO, ARTIST

The U.S. Army hires John Mauchly and J. Presper Eckert to build ENIAC.

1943

French marine scientist Jacques Cousteau invents the aqualung (scuba).

Scientists used IBM punch cards to enter information on ENIAC. Each card contained a small bit of information, called data. It took thousands of punch cards to input the data needed to achieve a result. Weeks passed before the punch cards could solve a simple calculation.

Despite ENIAC's limitations, the U.S. Army used it to help design the hydrogen bomb. Such a bomb is capable of causing major explosions and widespread destruction. ENIAC was also used to help forecast weather, design wind tunnels, and study cosmic rays—particles from outer space that enter Earth's atmosphere. Within ten years, however, the computer went into retirement. Today, ENIAC's many parts are on display in various museums around the world.

1947

Eckert and Mauchly patent ENIAC (left).

Jackie Robinson becomes the first African American to play on a major-league baseball team.

CHAPTER FOUR

CHIPS, THE INTERNET, AND PCS

In the early 1950s, banks and businesses slowly began to realize how useful computers were. The U.S. government used computers for military activities, the census, and tracking purchases and payments. But at that point, the idea of people owning their own computers was laughable. Ken Olsen, president of Digital Equipment, said, "There is no reason for any individual to have a computer at home."

During the late 1940s, the computer business leaped into a smaller-better-faster mode. In 1947, Walter Brittain was studying the effect of moisture on a small silicon circuit. Silicon is a chemical that is used to make glass and electronic parts. Brittain was growing frustrated with his experiment and he dumped the circuit into a Thermos of water. Suddenly, he realized that the

The computer business enters
a smaller-better-faster mode.

LATE **1940s**

The Cold War begins.

circuit was performing just the way he wanted. When underwater, it increased the signal being sent.

Brittain and fellow scientists William Shockley and John Bardeen worked together to develop the **transistor.** Their invention led to smaller components and reduced the need for vacuum tubes. ENIAC's 18,000 tubes became a thing of the past.

1958: THE SILICON CHIP

The 1950s and '60s saw huge advances in the computer business. In 1956, IBM introduced the RAMAC 305. This computer—powerful for the 1950s—had a **hard drive** that could store 5 megabytes.

A byte is a tiny piece of information housed in a

| 1947 | The transistor is developed. | 1949 | A description of Simon, the first true PC, appears in a book. |
| | *The Diary of a Young Girl* by Anne Frank is published. | | The People's Republic of China is founded as a communist government. |

computer's memory. The storage space in a computer's memory is usually measured in kilobytes (KB) or megabytes (MB). One KB is equal to 1,024 bytes, and 1 MB is equal to 1,024 KB. Compared to the storage space on today's computers, 5 MB is not that much.

In 1958, Texas Instruments built the first silicon chip. Because it even further reduced the need for so many electrical components, the tiny chip made the smaller-better-faster dream a reality.

At about this time, some companies offered people the opportunity to build their computers at home. One of the earliest products available was a HeathKit, which sold for $200.

IBM introduces the RAMAC 305, which has a hard drive with a total capacity of 5 MB.

1956

Tunisia and Morocco gain independence from France.

Texas Instruments builds the first silicon chip (above).

1958

The first cardiac pacemaker is implanted by Swedish surgeon Ake Senning and engineer Rune Elmqvist.

Honeywell, which specialized in home-heating devices called thermostats, jumped into the computer market. Its Honeywell Kitchen Computer sold for $10,600. It even had a built-in cutting board so that kitchen counter space was never wasted.

The book *How to Build a Working Digital Computer* was published in 1967. The book gave directions for making a computer from items commonly found at home—tin cans, bits of wire, and paper clips. The resulting computer earned the nickname The Paper Clip Computer.

1969: ARPANET DEBUTS

For the past forty years, the flurry of computer advances has been amazing. A few select events, however, set the stage for

1969

ARPANET, the granddaddy of the Internet, is developed.

Neil Armstrong and Buzz Aldrin become the first people to walk on the Moon.

modern computing. They include ARPANET, the Internet, PCs, and laptops. These advances are older than you think!

The granddaddy of today's Internet was ARPANET. During the 1960s, the U.S. military wanted to improve communications and get better use out of its computers. ARPA—the Advanced Research Projects Agency—accomplished this in 1969. It succeeded in linking the military's various computers to create the first online network.

The idea of Internet use by ordinary people came in 1973. At the time, "ordinary" people referred to individuals who could program a computer. Today, Internet service providers (ISPs) such as America Online, Inc. (AOL) and Microsoft Network (MSN) allow most people to access the

The idea of Internet use by ordinary people is introduced.

1973

Construction begins on the World Trade Center (right) in New York.

Internet. But in 1973, widespread Internet access was still a distant dream.

PCs first appeared during the early 1970s. Early models included the Altair and the Mark 8. Apple—a company that was first run out of the founder's garage—offered the Apple I in 1976. IBM had no interest in PCs until small computers were already popular. IBM provided nothing new, but they were the first to use the term *PC* in 1981.

Another advancement that occurred at about that time was the creation of the laptop computer. Adam Osborne developed the first "real" laptop in 1981. The Osborne 1 had a 5-inch (12.5-centimeter) screen. It also featured a modem port and a battery pack (a

1976

Apple introduces the Apple 1 (left).

A deadly earthquake in China kills more than 600,000 people.

rechargeable battery used in smaller computers). The modem port allowed Osborne 1 to communicate with other computers using telephone lines.

In 1983, Apple introduced the Macintosh. Today, Macs are the computer of choice in printing, moviemaking, and graphic arts. Mac Powerbooks came on the market in 1991. These computers weighed only 5 pounds (2.3 kg) and were relatively inexpensive.

IBM PCs and **clones** using Windows have now taken over the small computer market. IBM-style computers are currently the most common computers on the world market.

The first laptop (right) is built and weighs 24 pounds (11 kg).

Sandra Day O'Connor becomes the first woman on the U.S. Supreme Court.

CHAPTER FIVE

ADVENTURES IN CYBERSPACE

For the computer world, the year 2000 (Y2K) could have been a disaster. Computer designers never considered what would happen when the year turned from 1999 to 2000. Computers that worked with four-digit years (2000) had no problems. Computers operating on two-digit year abbreviations (00) faced big trouble.

Suppose a bank checked out how long someone paid against a loan. With the two-digit dating system, the math might read 00-96=-96. The *00* stands for the year 2000, and *96* refers to 1996—the year the loan was taken out. Unfortunately, *00-96=-96* implies that the borrower had gone 96 years without paying. Computer companies expected the worst—but it didn't happen. Luckily, all the problems were fixed before Y2K began.

1999	2000

Panic rises about possible Y2K problems.

Bertrand Piccard and Brian Jones successfully circle the world in a hot-air balloon.

George W. Bush and Al Gore run in the U.S. presidential election.

In the early 2000s, buyers continue to want the same type of computer—small, cheap, fast—and with added capabilities. Today, people can record home movies and edit them on their computers. They can download music off the Internet.

By 2000, the **search engine** Google could access more than 1 billion pages from the World Wide Web. In December 2000, more than 15 billion text messages flew through cyberspace—that empty region flowing with **bits** and bytes. The following year, 9.8 billion electronic messages were sent daily. More than 167 million people in the United States had Internet access. Worldwide, nearly 461 million people had Internet connections.

"EVEN THE COMPUTER INDUSTRY [BUSINESS] FAILED TO SEE THE IMPORTANCE OF THE INTERNET, BUT THAT'S NOT SAYING MUCH. LET'S FACE IT, THE COMPUTER INDUSTRY FAILED TO SEE THAT THE CENTURY WOULD END."
— DOUGLAS ADAMS, AUTHOR OF *THE HITCHHIKER'S GUIDE TO THE GALAXY*

2001

Nearly 461 million people worldwide are connected to the Internet.

Mir Space Station (right) re-enters the Earth's atmosphere.

2005: WHERE ARE COMPUTERS HEADED?

The future of computers is filled with vast possibilities. New ideas develop daily—new technology follows close behind. The computer you purchase today is already out-dated because newer, faster, cheaper technology develops even as you leave the store.

Karel Capek first used the term *robot* in his play *R.U.R.* Little did he imagine the role that robots would play in our lives. The car you ride in, the TV you watch, the CD you listen to, and even the food you eat are a result of robotics.

Industrial robots create parts and put together today's cars and TVs. Robotics are used to reproduce CDs by the

2002

Honda debuts its humanoid robot Asimo (left) in the United States.

A terrorist bombing on the Indonesian island of Bali kills hundreds.

millions. Robots pick, clean, and process vegetables and fruits. They pack, store, sort, and move food through warehouses.

Manufacturers expect computers to become even more important to home entertainment. Computers will tape, play, and edit music, movies, and TV programs. They will link humans, TVs, and telephones.

Soon, your computer will know how to respond to your voice. You'll sit at your desk and say, "Computer, find research on Thomas Jefferson." The computer will spit out quotes, dates, and endless facts about Jefferson. Most computers already automatically fix your grammar, spelling, and punctuation, but you'll still have to write that research paper yourself.

ROBOTICS

In 2004, the first "nursebot" was introduced to the public. "Pearl" helps care for the elderly. She reminds her patients to eat breakfast or to take their medicine. She helps those who can't walk to get around more easily. The first Pearl cost $100,000 to build. It will be awhile before more nursebots can be produced at a cheaper price.

2003

Aniéres, Switzerland, holds an official online election.

Forces lead by the United States invade Iraq.

2004

The first nursebot is introduced to the public.

The Olympics are held in Athens, Greece.

abacus (AB-uh-kuhss)
An abacus is a device made of counters that can be moved along rods or grooves; it is used for adding and subtracting. The Chinese used an abacus to determine money owed for goods sold.

bits (BITZ)
Bits are single units of information. A modern computer processes millions of bits every minute.

calculation (kal-kyuh-LAY-shun)
A calculation is the process of figuring out a math problem. Scientists performed many calculations to figure out the distance between the Earth and the Moon.

census (SEN-suhss)
A census is an official population count. The government hired Herman Hollerith to build an electronic machine that used punch cards to count the U.S. Census.

clones (KLOHNZ)
Clones are scientifically produced duplicates. Dell and Gateway computers are IBM clones.

hard drive (HARD DRIVE)
A hard drive is located inside a computer and is used for storing data. RAMAC 305 had a hard drive that could store 5 MB.

patent (PAT-uhnt)
A patent is a piece of paper from the government that gives a person or company the rights to make or sell a new invention. John Mauchly and J. Presper Eckert received a patent for ENIAC.

prototypes (PROH-tuh-tipes)
Prototypes are the first models of an invention. Pascal made fifty different prototypes of his calculator, and it still couldn't add French money.

search engine (SURCH EN-juhn)
A search engine is a computer site that finds information based on words or phrases that you type in. Google is a popular search engine.

silicon chips (SIL-uh-kuhn CHIPS)
Silicon chips are small devices that contain electronic circuits. Today's silicon chips carry billions of electronic messages.

slide rule (SLIDE ROOL)
A slide rule is a device that consists of a ruler and a movable middle section; it is used for making complex calculations. Since computers have become popular, math and science students no longer use slide rules.

transistor (tran-ZISS-tur)
A transistor is an electronic device used to connect circuits. Transistors made vacuum tubes unnecessary.

AT THE LIBRARY

Nonfiction

*Collier, Bruce, and James MacLachlan. *Charles Babbage and the Engines of Perfection*. New York: Oxford University Press, 1998.

Cook, Peter, and Scott Manning. *Why Doesn't My Floppy Disk Flop?: And Other Kids' Computer Questions Answered by the CompuDudes*. New York: John Wiley, 1999.

*McCartney, Scott. *ENIAC: The Triumphs and Tragedies of the World's First Computer*. New York: Walker, 1999.

Raatma, Lucia. *Safety on the Internet*. Chanhassen, Minn.: The Child's World, 2005.

Sherman, Josepha. *The History of the Personal Computer*. New York: Franklin Watts, 2003.

Fiction

Regan, Dian Curtis, and Melissa Sweet (illustrator). *Monsters in Cyberspace*. New York: Henry Holt & Company, 1997.

* *Books marked with a star are challenge reading material for those reading above grade level.*

ON THE WEB

Visit our home page for lots of links about computers:
http://www.childsworld.com/links

Note to Parents, Teachers, and Librarians:
We routinely check our Web links to make sure they're safe, active sites—so encourage your readers to check them out!

PLACES TO VISIT OR CONTACT

American Computer Museum
2304 N. Seventh Ave., Suite B
Bozeman, MT 59715
406/582-1288

Cahners Computer Place
Museum of Science, Science Park
Boston, MA 02114
617/589-0180

Computer History Museum
1401 N. Shoreline Boulevard
Mountain View, CA 94043
650/810-1010

ABOUT THE AUTHOR

BARBARA SOMERVILL IS THE AUTHOR OF MANY BOOKS FOR CHILDREN. SHE LOVES LEARNING AND SEES EVERY WRITING PROJECT AS A CHANCE TO LEARN NEW INFORMATION OR GAIN A NEW UNDERSTANDING. MS. SOMERVILL GREW UP IN NEW YORK STATE, BUT HAS ALSO LIVED IN TORONTO, CANADA; CANBERRA, AUSTRALIA; CALIFORNIA; AND SOUTH CAROLINA. SHE CURRENTLY LIVES WITH HER HUSBAND IN SIMPSONVILLE, SOUTH CAROLINA.